BEYOND BURNOUT

how to find rest in a restless world

Mike Novotny

with bonus Bible study by Dr. Bruce Becker

Published by Straight Talk Books
P.O. Box 301, Milwaukee, WI 53201
800.661.3311 • timeofgrace.org

Copyright © 2024 Time of Grace Ministry

All rights reserved. This publication may not be copied, photocopied, reproduced, translated, or converted to any electronic or machine-readable form in whole or in part, except for brief quotations, without prior written approval from Time of Grace Ministry.

Scripture is taken from THE HOLY BIBLE, NEW INTERNATIONAL VERSION®, NIV®. Copyright © 1973, 1978, 1984, 2011 by Biblica, Inc.® Used by permission. All rights reserved worldwide.

Printed in the United States of America

ISBN: 978-1-949488-88-3

TIME OF GRACE *is a registered mark of Time of Grace Ministry.*

CONTENTS

INTRODUCTION
5

CHAPTER 1
Physical Burnout, Physical Rest
11

CHAPTER 2
Spiritual Burnout, Spiritual Rest
43

CHAPTER 3
Emotional Burnout, Emotional Rest
73

CONCLUDING THOUGHTS
105

INTRODUCTION

Although video games are all the rage, do you still like playing board games? Since there are different genres or types of board games, you might answer this question differently depending on what type of game we're talking about. At least I would.

Some games involve the rolling of dice, like Yahtzee or Monopoly. The winner of dice-based games is determined in part by the roll of the dice, by chance. Other board games determine a winner based on the consensus of the players playing the game, like Apples to Apples or Consensus. In these games, the participants pick the winner. Majority rules. A third type of board game is strategy based, like chess or checkers and newer games like Catan, Ticket to Ride, or Carcassonne. Personally, I prefer strategy games to those that involve chance. And I prefer *never* to play games that pick the winner on the basis of consensus. How about you?

No matter what kind of board games you like to play, every game has rules, instructions for how to play the game, and a method for determining the winner. So who determines the rules of the game? Those playing the game? I don't think so. It's the creator of the game who determines the rules. The creator of the game also determines how to play it, in other words how the play-by-play rhythm flows. And the creator decides how someone wins the game. The creator of the game determines everything about the game that he or she created.

What's true for something as insignificant as a board game is also true for something as important as the universe and world in which we live. The rules that govern the universe and how it functions have all been determined by the Creator of the universe.

In the first two chapters of the first book of the Bible, Genesis, we read about the creation of the universe by our Creator. When we read these chapters, it becomes clear that our God built specific rules and rhythms into his creation.

On the first day of creation, we see how our Creator established a *daily* rhythm:

> **And God said, "Let there be light," and there was light. God saw that the light was good, and he separated the light from the darkness. God called the light "day," and the darkness he called "night." And there was evening, and there was morning— the first day. (Genesis 1:3-5)**

The *daily* rhythm that God created included a period of darkness, which God called night, and a period of light,

INTRODUCTION

which God called day. The period of darkness was designed for rest, and the period of light was designed for work and activity. This *daily* rhythm has happened every day since the beginning of time.

On day four of creation, we learn specifically how the Creator designed the periods of darkness and light to function:

> **And God said, "Let there be lights in the vault of the sky to separate the day from the night, and let them serve as signs to mark sacred times, and days and years, and let them be lights in the vault of the sky to give light on the earth." And it was so. God made two great lights—the greater light to govern the day and the lesser light to govern the night. He also made the stars. God set them in the vault of the sky to give light on the earth, to govern the day and the night, and to separate light from darkness. And God saw that it was good. And there was evening, and there was morning—the fourth day.**
> (Genesis 1:14-19)

In addition to the *daily* rhythm of day and night that occurs as the result of God creating the earth to rotate on its axis, our Creator designed *monthly* and *annual* rhythms too. God created a monthly moon cycle (new moon, waxing crescent, first quarter, waxing gibbous, full moon, waning gibbous, last quarter, and waning crescent) that repeats every 29.5 days. God also created the earth to revolve around the sun approximately every 365 days and then tilted the earth's axis so that we would enjoy four different seasons—spring, summer, fall, and winter. The daily, monthly, and annual rhythms were all part of the Creator's design for the world in which we live. And remember, the Creator is the one who makes the rules and determines how his creation functions.

The Creator also created a *weekly* rhythm that we especially want to focus on in this book: **"By the seventh day God had finished the work he had been doing; so on the seventh day he rested from all his work. Then God blessed the seventh day and made it holy, because on it he rested from all the work of creating that he had done"** (Genesis 2:2,3).

Our Creator-God worked for six days creating the beautiful world and universe in which we live. Then on day seven, he rested. Six days of work followed by a day of rest. That's our Creator's design for a *weekly* rhythm. This was God's design for himself during creation week as well as his design for us.

So what are we at risk of if we don't follow God's *daily* or *weekly* rhythms? It's called burnout. Burnout is the result of disrupting the rhythms that God established for us at creation.

In chapter 1 of this book, Pastor Mike will summarize the goal of his teaching on burnout. It will set the stage for the rest of the book, so let's consider his words here:

INTRODUCTION

We're going to talk about burnout from a physical perspective, a spiritual perspective, and an emotional perspective. And for me, the goal is to help you run your race of faith. I chose that verb intentionally—*run*. I don't want you to walk. It's true; some people in the church are lazy, they're unreliable, or they quit when things get hard. That's bad, but I'm not going to talk about that.

Instead, I want to talk about the people who aren't running their races; they're sprinting at an unsustainable pace. They're pushing so hard yet barely getting by, and it will catch up with them. If this is you with too much on your plate, my goal is to slow you down. Not too much but enough so you can run a race of faith with peace and joy and love for other people in Jesus' name.

In the chapters of this book, Pastor Mike will address three types of burnout—physical, spiritual, and emotional. Then at the end of each chapter in the "Digging Deeper" sections, I'll help you look further into what the Bible has to say about burnout and rest.
This book will help you live in God's rhythm.

—Dr. Bruce Becker

CHAPTER 1
Physical Burnout, Physical Rest

It struck me recently that the American culture in which I live sets us up, chews us up, and then burns us out. I'm not being weak and whiny. I'm actually thinking about current times compared to other times in the past, the place and the culture in which I live. When you combine those two things—place and culture—you might agree with me that American culture sets us up, chews us up, and then burns us out.

It's a culture in which we're not just busy, but as the average American says, "We're busy, busy, busy!" It's not just occasional periods when we're rushing and behind and overwhelmed with everything on our to-do lists. It's when it's all the time, not the exception but the norm. The stress of having lots to do turns into anxiety: "What if I can't do all this?" That turns into feeling overwhelmed: "I'm never going to get this done." And that turns into burnout for both body and soul.

BEYOND BURNOUT

THE RECIPE FOR BURNOUT

We live in a culture that has the perfect recipe for burning people out. Here it is: First, we live in a modern culture. You might not think of this because you live within it, but in the days of Moses or in the days of Jesus or in the days of George Washington, before there were light bulbs and laptops, most of life was governed by the simple rhythms that God built into creation. There was day; there was night. There was light when you could do your work; there was darkness when you couldn't. There were times when you had to walk to talk to other people. When you went back home, you were physically separated from others. Most people didn't violate that physical separation. If you were a farmer and sunset came, there wasn't much farming to do.

But times have changed. Thomas Edison gave us the light bulb, so we aren't bound by light and darkness. The internet and laptops were invented, so work doesn't have to stay at work. If you want to talk to your boss, you don't have to wait until Monday morning; you can grab your cell, text, grab your laptop, or you can email. The boundaries and barriers that prevent burnout are totally off in a modern culture.

Do you own a smartphone? If you do, your manager, pastor, brother, sister, son, daughter, mother, father, next-door neighbor, and a million marketers can call you and text you and ring you and ding you and ping you and DM you and get your attention. When you think it's your day off, it's never your day off as long as that device is in

PHYSICAL BURNOUT, PHYSICAL REST

your hand. You can always be reached. Welcome to the modern world.

Then COVID happened. More and more people who used to leave work at work now shifted work to their homes. It used to be that the papers and the stuff and the devices that you used to do your work were far away on the other side of town. Now it's all in your office, which is in your home. The modern world has made it so easy to work all the time and so difficult to step away and rest.

Then there are the devices that convince us that rest looks like sitting down and scrolling. Based on everything that neurologists and doctors tell us, sitting and scrolling is not good for providing peace and rest for our hearts. Internet and social media use increases, if not skyrockets, levels of anxiety and depression. We deal with it every single day. There are no barriers and no boundaries, just constant work and a very rare ability to truly rest.

Are you stressed yet? Modern culture is just the first ingredient! Now combine that with the second ingredient: our American culture. Not every culture shares America's passion/idolatry for bigger and better, progress, and profit. I read a study that said the average American worker works over 400 more hours a year than the average German worker.[1] Forgive the stereotype, but I never thought of Germans as lazy. But the average American puts in ten more weeks of full-time work. Compared to the average Japanese worker,

[1] "Average Annual Hours Actually Worked Per Worker," OECD, accessed December 3, 2023, https://data-viewer.oecd.org/?chartId=312.

the average American worker puts in over 200 more hours every single year. If you live in the U.S., you don't realize how much Americans work. Other countries have paid maternity and paternity leave policies. There's no federal law guaranteeing these sorts of paid leaves in America. Others have huge cultural times when people don't work; they take holiday. Not in America. We work because we want bigger and better.

I recently read an article that said since the 1940s, the average American family has gotten smaller; families had more kids in the past than they do today.[2] But on average those bigger families lived in homes that were—are you ready for this?—983 square feet. Have you ever driven around the original downtown of a city and seen the one-car garages and small homes? Those held bigger families than ours do today. Welcome to America; things are bigger. These days we need a two- or three-car garage for all our stuff. We need a shed in the backyard for all our toys. We need walk-in closets. Who has enough closets? We have more storage units than we know what to do with. We've accelerated our need for consumption and materialism, and in the process, we've had to work more and more hours to afford it, to fill it, to pay for it, and to care for it. This is the American culture.

It's not just our houses that are bigger; it's also the callings that we have in life. A hundred years ago, what was

2. Taylor Covington, "Supersized: Americans Are Living in Bigger Houses With Fewer People," *The Zebra*, Updated January 2, 2023, https://www.thezebra.com/resources/home/median-home-size-in-us/.

PHYSICAL BURNOUT, PHYSICAL REST

expected of a pastor like me? To preach the Bible and show up when someone had a question or was sick. Yep. That has gotten bigger. Now there's the church website and the church social media, and you've got to make videos and edit this and that. You've got to know how to do YouTube and Facebook ads to reach your community. You need events like Trunk or Treat and kid events for Christmas and Easter. There's stuff needed for Sunday school and the teen group and the moms' group and all the other groups.

I bet that's happened to you too. One hundred years ago, what would your profession have been like compared to now?

If you're a couple about to get married in modern America, there are some big expectations of what you need to do to plan a wedding! I would not want to be a new mom in modern America where being a mom only is looked down on by some people. It's as if you have to have a side hustle on Etsy or a part-time job or a full-time job or else you're not pulling your weight as an American woman. We live in a culture that pushes and pushes and pushes. Students can't just be students; now they need language credits and music lessons. One percent of kid athletes used to be in traveling clubs; now every kid is in a club and goes to a camp and has to compete fiercely just to make the varsity team. Sports are different, music is different, motherhood is different, ministry is different, everything is different. Welcome to America!

Are you stressed yet? Because I'm not done. There's one last ingredient in our recipe for burnout. It's not just modern culture or American culture. Finally, many of us are part of a Christian culture. And Christian culture, especially in America, has gotten bigger and faster too.

We encourage people to go to church and to take time to work on their faith and read their Bibles. And we encourage them to do this not just once in a while but every single day, maybe at the start of the day and the end of the day. Don't forget that prayer is valuable. Fasting can be valuable. Journaling can be valuable. Ooh, you should volunteer, so get a T-shirt that says, "You First." Speaking of that, put other people first too by serving your neighbor. Which one of your neighbors? Both of your neighbors. All of your neighbors. Everyone is your neighbor, right? Jesus was sacrificial and selfless, and he served people. So if you're going to be a Christian, you should be sacrificial and selfless and serve people. Say yes when somebody needs help. If someone's on the side of the road, stop and fix their tire. If your mother needs someone to move her furniture, go up and help and honor your mom. There are all these commands and to-dos. We think that's what Christian culture looks like.

Modern + American + Christian = Phew! That's a recipe for burnout.

WHAT TYPE OF PERSON ARE YOU?

Another factor of burnout can come from the way we are wired. It's a good part of our personalities that without

PHYSICAL BURNOUT, PHYSICAL REST

real intention can go too far and burn us out. Do you know someone who's fairly compassionate? They feel others feelings in times of need. Compassionate people are amazing, and compassionate people have a hard time saying no, don't they? Are you one of those people? It's like your heart hurts so much for people who are hurting that you want to be there for them. You want to be the one who shows up. And in a digital age when everyone can ring you and ding you and ping you, when you can see everyone's problems on Facebook and Instagram, you overextend yourself. There's not enough energy in your body or hours in the day.

Do you know someone who's really responsible? Are you one of those people? You say you're going to do something, and you do it. That can be dangerous when you've already committed to some previous tasks, but then you get interrupted by new and extra tasks. Since you do what you say you'll do, you have a hard time saying, "I'm sorry, but life got too busy. I'm going to have to back out." Instead you say, "I have to follow through; I have to be a person of my word."

Do you know someone who's competitive? Are you one of those people? You get really grouchy when you lose a board game at Christmas. Like me, you love to compete, love to push, love to excel, and love to set records and make resolutions and then follow through and break those records. That means there's always a next level to get to. You read 10 books last year. How about 15 books this year? How about 20? How about 2 books a month? How about a book every single week? There are just more and bigger and better things to do.

There is a current moving so fast in modern culture that unless you swim against it, it will burn you out. It will fill up your schedule and beyond. It will push you past the point where you want to be. And here is why that matters so much to me as a pastor: because I've noticed in my life and in the lives of others that when you and I are burned out, exhausted, and overwhelmed, we are rarely like Jesus. We can make it to church, squeeze in some Bible reading and religious stuff, but are we joyful like Jesus? Do we have the peace of God that Jesus had? Are we patient and kind? And in my experience, it doesn't matter how much you go to church or how much you read your Bible. If you are overcommitted, it is so hard to produce the fruit of the Spirit.

DO YOU SPRINT AT AN UNSUSTAINABLE PACE?

A Christian woman goes to a very important meeting one day, and she's 15 minutes early. She goes to the same meeting another day, and she's 5 minutes late. In which situation is she bound to be more like Jesus when a sweet old lady is driving 17 miles per hour or honoring a school zone? It's not what happens; it's the pace in which it happens. Every stoplight becomes a frustration. Every city planner who set the speed limit is stupid; why is it 25 miles per hour? Like this woman, you get mad when you wouldn't usually be mad. You're impatient when you wouldn't usually be impatient. You don't have time for interruptions and sick kids and problems, right? When we are burned out and running, running, rushing, rushing, we actually lose some of the incredible blessings that come from being a Christian. Like the joy of being forgiven. Or the peace of knowing that God controls the universe. I'm not just concerned about your schedule; I'm concerned about your soul, the blessings it has, and the blessings that it gives.

That's why we're going to try and change that. We're going to talk about burnout from a physical perspective, a spiritual perspective, and an emotional perspective. And for me, the goal is to help you run your race of faith. I chose that verb intentionally—*run*. I don't want you to walk. It's true; some people in the church are lazy, they're unreliable, or they quit when things get hard. That's bad, but I'm not going to talk about that in this book.

Instead, I want to talk about the people who aren't running their races; they're sprinting at an unsustainable pace. They're pushing so hard yet barely getting by, and it will catch up with them. If this is you with too much on your plate, my goal is to slow you down. Not too much but enough so you can run a race of faith with peace and joy and love for other people in Jesus' name.

WHO MAKES THE RULES?

Now to get you one step closer to that, I want to start in the beginning. Literally. I want to teach you the first half of the first verse of the first chapter of the first book of the Bible. In that half of a verse is a truth that is actually so obvious when you think about it but so important for your life. The first half of Genesis 1:1 says this: **"In the beginning God created."** God created. Verb = *created*. Subject = *God*. Object = *you* . . . and the heavens and the earth and everything that they contain. In the beginning, the Bible says, God created.

I had a chance to go from cover to cover in the Bible and read every verse that uses words like *create, created,* and *creation*. What I learned is that the Bible almost exclusively reserves the act of creation for God. It talks about humans. It talks about animals. But God is always labeled as the Creator. The roles are never switched; we don't create God. We don't even create from the Bible's perspective. We are a creation that God created.

Here's what that implies. It implies that the Creator creates the rules. The One who creates something gets to decide how that something works, how it functions. If you're a designer of a device or a product, you get to determine the details of what makes it work and what makes it break. Do you agree? If you and I run an athletic company and we make those bouncy balls that kids use on playgrounds, we make them in a certain way with a certain material so they bounce. On the other hand, if you and I work at a china company and produce and create really fine china, we can't swap a china plate with a bouncy ball. One bounces; the other doesn't. Kids don't get to decide how things work; the Creator gets to decide how things work.

So in the beginning, the Bible says, God created everything, and that means God gets to decide the rules of how everything works, what makes something thrive, and what makes it wither and die. God made fish with gills to live in the water. He made beagles with legs to run on the land. He made eagles with wings to fly in the sky. And the fish and the beagles and eagles don't get to decide for themselves how their bodies work. They simply follow the rules that God created for their bodies. So if Fred the fish says, "I'm going to be a beagle today" and jumps out of the sea into a park, what happens to Fred? Fred is dead, right? The Creator creates the rules. If Benny the beagle says, "I'm not a beagle; I'm an eagle," and he jumps off a cliff, what happens to the beagle? Well, he's not an eagle. He tries to fly, and then he dies because the creation doesn't get to make up its own rules about what it wants to be. There's no "my truth" in creation; there's just the truth with which the Creator created it. Do you agree with me so far?

Now guess who else that applies to? You and me. As a part of the creation, we don't get to decide the rules for our bodies. Scientists and doctors can study how an eagle works and why it flies, neurologists and nutritionists can study how our bodies work, what makes our hearts work, and when our brains are functioning at top level, but they can't make the rules. Here's how you sleep, but you don't get to decide if you need sleep or not. That's how God made you. You can learn about food and nutrition, but you don't get to decide what makes you run at peak performance.

That's been built into you by the Creator who created the rules. Your body needs exercise whether you decide it does or not. The Creator creates the rules, and God created you with a need to eat and to move and to sleep.

I'm guessing you already knew that. You can't fly. You don't climb up to your roof and jump off like an eagle in order to fly where you want to go. No, your body wasn't made for that. But if I could push you a little bit, I would ask this: Does your lifestyle reflect an obedience to the physical rules that the Creator created? If I looked at your schedule, your lifestyle, and your habits and compared them to what experts have found (here's how people like you work), how much obedience and how much rebellion to those rules would I see?

WHEN WE FORGET WHO MAKES THE RULES

I think one of the problems that we often run into in the modern world is that because culture pushes and pushes, we sometimes forget we don't get to decide how this works. It has already been decided for us. When you and I ignore that, we put ourselves on a path to almost certain burnout.

Here are three things that happen. First of all, we compromise. We know the rules of how the human body works, but we fudge them just a little bit, sort of like when we drive 32 in a 25-mile-per-hour zone. We know the doctors and experts say we should sleep about seven to nine hours, but

PHYSICAL BURNOUT, PHYSICAL REST

we sleep less. And we know we should be careful with sugar, alcohol, and desserts because they aren't good for the body. They mess with our hearts, and our brains don't function like they should. We crash, we can't stay awake, we're not alert, but we overdo it anyway. We know exercise is good for our hearts, memories, minds, and sleep habits, but we don't exercise. Have you seen those stickers on the backs of cars that read 0.0, as in I ran 0.0 miles? We don't do any exercise. We know there are rules—and I'm not talking about fad diets or super details—we know there's a general way the human body functions, but we compromise.

Next, we compensate. We start to reap what we sow. We don't get enough sleep, so we're tired. In the morning, we don't reach for a cup of coffee; we fill up a whole pot. We have an energy drink and a granola bar for breakfast. We're not awake for the first hour of school because we've been up late playing games with friends. We can't function like we're supposed to function, so we compensate. We push a really stressful pace at work and then bring work home. There's no downtime. We check emails until the time we go to bed. We can't sleep, so we compensate. We reach for a drink, maybe two. We pour whiskey and make it pretty stiff. We need a glass of wine. We need some extra time. There's a pill, maybe two, just to sleep. We go to the doctor to get some unnecessary medications to compensate for the compromises we've made. Or maybe we just know we're always stressed, always on edge, so we take a vacation. Sometimes a vacation is just compensation, right? We're always stressed, so this will fix it. We don't slow the pace of our lives but instead slap a vacation on it for seven to ten days. We think an all-inclusive binge is going to make it better.

We compromise, compensate, and then finally, we crash. It rarely happens right in the beginning; sometimes it doesn't happen in the middle. But sooner or later, we crash. We hit a wall and have a physical breakdown. It's a panic attack. It's the depression you've never experienced before. It's as if you find it hard to function or just get numb. You go to church, but you feel nothing. You read your Bible, but you don't get anything out of it. You crash when you get home. There's no energy left, so you take it out on the people you love the most. It's not just your heart and your lungs and your muscles that get hurt when you compromise and compensate; it's your soul and the precious lives of the ones you love.

So here's a question. We know that when we're really hungry, we can get angry; there's a name for that—hangry. We know there's a connection between physical habits and character choices. My question for you is this: Is it possible that some of the things you're struggling with regarding your character are not some mysterious spiritual battle but just a physical reality? You've pushed too hard? You've used up your calories on all these things, and now there's none left for the energy to follow Jesus and love his people?

PHYSICAL BURNOUT, PHYSICAL REST

I LEARNED THE HARD WAY

About a decade ago, I ran a marathon up in Green Bay, Wisconsin. I tried my best to qualify for the Boston Marathon. It required a time of three hours flat for a man my age. There was just one problem with my goal: I was not personally qualified to qualify for the Boston Marathon. I hadn't trained. I hadn't run. I wasn't ready, not even close. My lungs weren't ready for three hours, my legs weren't ready, and my ligaments weren't ready, but for some crazy reason, I got to the starting line and said, "You know what? I'm going to qualify for the Boston Marathon. It's all in your head, Mike. Just run and don't stop."

So that's what I did. I found the pacesetter. He had a little sign that said, "Three hours." I said, "I'm not going to let this guy go. I'm going to run with him. Running is painful, but it will be over in three hours. You'll be fine. You can rest later this week." Boom! The gun went off, and I ran like a gazelle, poetry in motion. I ran with this guy at a three-hour marathon pace for the first mile and then the second mile, and then two miles turned into four miles, six miles, and eight miles. I ran ten miles at that pace, and then I kept running. I hit mile 11, 12, 13, and 14. I was qualifying for Boston at mile 15. I ran with this guy for 16 miles at a three-hour marathon pace. Are you impressed?

You shouldn't be because a marathon is not 16 miles long. It's 26.2 miles long. At mile 16 I remember where it happened. Boom! I smashed into a proverbial wall 10.2 miles from the finish line. I went from running like a gazelle to looking like your grandma after double hip replacement. I went from sprinting to walking. I didn't just hit the wall; I left my outline in it because I hit it so hard. And for the next 10.2 miles, I cried and cramped and limped my way to the finish line. I remember at one point near Lambeau Field as I was shuffling along, I saw a half-finished Gatorade on the curb. I was so thirsty, and I stopped and looked at the germ-covered, half-drunk Gatorade that had been in the sun for way too long. I reached over to get it, and my whole body cramped. I wasn't sure if I could get up from this position.

What did I do? I tried to act like the Creator instead of the creation. I thought there were no rules for lungs and legs and ligaments. I was going to figure it out as I went. I thought I didn't need to respect how much I'd trained or what my body was capable of. I figured I was just going to do it. I tried to rewrite the rules, and then I had to reap what I had sown.

Now I'm not sure where you are today. Maybe you're at mile eight of that kind of pace and feeling pretty good. You're doing it. You're on five hours of sleep, skipping workouts, and you're not dead yet. You're killing it at work, doing more than you've ever done; things are fine. But I want to tell you from the experience of people who are just as smart and just as driven and just as compassionate as you, it doesn't matter if you're a nurse or a dad or a pastor. It doesn't matter what you do, you are part of the creation. You are not the Creator. The Creator creates the rules.

PHYSICAL BURNOUT, PHYSICAL REST

IT'S TIME FOR A BREAK

Let's talk about Jesus. Two thousand years ago Jesus took on human flesh and had a body like yours with lungs and legs. If your impression is that because Christ was so loving and so selfless, which he was, that for 33 years he worked 20-hour days serving everyone he met until he hit a wall and died on a cross, you would be dead wrong. Jesus had seasons of intense work where he was up early and up late, where he poured himself out into people's needs. But to assume that was the way Jesus normally lived would actually be a biblical and doctrinal mistake.

Let me show you a fascinating passage from the book of Luke. In Luke 5:15,16 it says, **"Crowds of people came to hear** [Jesus]." There were hundreds, maybe thousands, of people. They came **"to be healed of their sicknesses."** They were sick, struggling, and desperate for a miracle. Notice the next word: **"But."** You would think crowds of people came to be healed, *and* Jesus healed them. Crowds of people needed a relief from their sicknesses; *therefore*, Jesus healed them. But that's not what the passage says. Crowds of people came. **"But Jesus often withdrew to lonely places and prayed."** Isn't that fascinating? He worked to love people, and before the work was even done, he withdrew. Some people say you've got to work until the job is done. Jesus said, "Nope." And don't miss the adverb. Jesus withdrew *"often."* This wasn't something he did once a year after a crazy time in ministry. He often, by himself and with his disciples, got away. He said, "We've loved these people for a long time; it's time for a break." Jesus' lifestyle and his constant and often habit was to withdraw to lonely places just to be with his heavenly Father and rest.

Jesus wasn't just part of our creation; he behaved like a creationist. It's a fascinating thought. He pushed hard, and then he pushed pause and didn't do work at all. Resting wasn't bad, and his Father wasn't mad. It didn't make Jesus selfish, lazy, or sinful.

Person in need: "What is Jesus doing? My mom has cancer; she needs to be healed!"

Disciple: "Yeah, Jesus knows. He's taking a nap. He's praying."

Person in need: "Well, how long?"

Disciple: "Probably all day."

Person in need: "Well, we need help."

Disciple: "*Mmm-hmm.* And Jesus needs rest."

If that's shocking to us, I wonder if our American culture has shaped our view of the Bible. Sometimes we pick just some of the things that Jesus did and some of the things the Scriptures say—work, serve, help—and we ignore the constant theme that God has a great place for his people just to be still and let him be God.

That's why I asked one of my former seminary professors a very important question. I'd been reading some of the calendar that God set for his ancient Jewish people in the Old Testament. There were religious holidays like Passover and Pentecost, and I noticed God gave his people a lot of

PHYSICAL BURNOUT, PHYSICAL REST

time off from their jobs. In today's world, if it's Christmas week, you might get one day or two from your employer. Not ancient Jews; they were given huge chunks of time. As I read, I noticed a chunk here and a chunk there. Then there was a day and two days over here. And then I thought, Jesus had to get all the way down to Jerusalem to celebrate some of those festivals, and he lived about three marathons away. He had to walk to Jerusalem; he didn't take a plane or a bus. How much time did it take him to leave behind the carpentry and the work and the chores at home just to be on the road, to be with family and friends, to be with God?

I sent an email to this professor I know with the subject line: "Jesus' Vacation Time." The professor, who is an expert in the Old Testament, wrote this to me: "An observant Jew in Jesus' day [someone who followed the Bible], would have had off 52 Sabbath Days [every Saturday], one day for the Festival of Purim, eight days for Passover, two days for Pentecost, two days for the Jewish New Year, one day for the Day of Atonement, nine days for the Feast of Tabernacles. In addition, Jewish men were supposed to show up in Jerusalem for Passover and Pentecost and Tabernacles, and it would have taken most of them quite some time to get there. Then the Old Testament says if you're a farmer, your farm is supposed to lie fallow, unfarmed, one year in every seven." In other words, God told Old Testament farmers to work hard for six years and then take an entire year off. A farmer sabbatical. If you're a farmer, can you even imagine that today? Also, the professor concluded, "Jesus' time off was time off. Not time to cram full of activities, digital distractions, and the NFL."

Isn't that amazing? When God created the calendar, he said, "I'm not mad, and you're not bad if you take huge chunks of time to rest. Work hard, but not for too long."

So here's my encouragement to you. God is not mad, and you are not a bad Christian if you rest. It's not selfish to take a break. It's the ancient rhythm of Jesus. If you're a mom who gets away for a half hour or half a day, it doesn't make you a bad mom. If you say no to a friend who wants to hang out or to another family gathering or to the pastor who needs someone to volunteer, it doesn't make you a bad person. It makes you a creationist. It means that you're someone who believes that God is the Creator and you can only do so much before things start to go very, very wrong.

The answer to burnout is to behave like a creationist. Don't just believe in creation. Behave like you're following the rules the Father built into your body. I hereby release those of you who are responsible and compassionate from the guilt and the necessity of needing to run. I hereby empower you in Jesus' name to sit, take a nap, do nothing, or pray. I'm allowing you today in Jesus' name to go to your cabin and not come back until Monday morning. I am giving you permission in the mighty name of Jesus to hear your phone bing and ping and ring and ignore it. I'm giving you full permission to rest, because Jesus wants a rest for your soul. I give this gift to you in Jesus' name, and all God's people said, "Amen!"

PHYSICAL BURNOUT, PHYSICAL REST

BUT, PASTOR MIKE . . .

Now you might be thinking, "No, Pastor Mike. If I rest, what happens the next day? If I put my phone away today, when I pick it up tomorrow, what's going to happen? I'm going to have twice as much to do. I'm going to be twice as stressed. You're telling me to take a break; don't work all the time. But if I actually rest, there's going to be more work, more phone calls, more emails, more stuff, more responsibilities, more boxes that aren't checked. I can't slow down."

If that's what you're thinking, you need to keep reading this book. In chapter 2 we'll lean in and listen to Jesus, who knows how deeply in our hearts we want people to be impressed by us and how we hate saying no and disappointing people. Jesus is going to fix that part of us and resize our schedules. As he said, **"Come to me, all you who are weary and burdened, and I will give you rest"** (Matthew 11:28).

But until then, I need to tell you one last thing about Jesus. And it's not an example of how he worked and rested; it's the love that he has for people who push too hard. You remember that really dumb marathon I ran? I hit mile 16 and was limping. There was a water stop really late in the race in front of a local news station. Some of the employees and the anchormen and women were handing out water and sports drinks. As I came limping up, I must have looked like the walking dead because a fairly recognizable anchorman started walking right for me. We had never met, but he handed me a sports drink filled with electrolytes, put his arm around my sweaty and exhausted shoulders, and walked with me. He told me that I was going to make it. He told me to drink up. He applauded and encouraged me. I didn't die before the end of the marathon.

I think that's a lot like Jesus. Maybe you've made foolish choices with your schedule; it's affected your body, your marriage, your relationships, and your faith. You can't go back and run a new pace. You're limping, trying to recover. Jesus would have every right to wag his finger and judge, but he doesn't. Instead, he sees you in all your exhaustion, and with love he puts that pierced hand around your shoulder in forgiveness and hands you his grace and mercy and says, "Drink up!" He promises with words of encouragement and grace that he's going to fill you with the Spirit, that he's going to give you wisdom and help you in your time of need. He doesn't trip you up. He doesn't come to condemn you or tell you to pick up the pace. Instead, he comes not just as an example but as your Redeemer and perfect Savior.

You and I believe that God is our Savior and our Creator. Today I pray that you believe in your salvation and with the help of God you behave like his creation.

DIGGING DEEPER

PHYSICAL BURNOUT

1. In this chapter Pastor Mike identifies three ingredients in the recipe for burnout.

   What are the three ingredients?
   -
   -
   -

   What is the underlying problem with each ingredient?
   -
   -
   -

   Give one example of how each ingredient has shown up in your own life or experience.
   -
   -
   -

2. In addition to the three ingredients that can lead to burnout, there are personality traits that can also contribute to burnout. Pastor Mike lists three: *being compassionate, being responsible,* and *being competitive.*

Give an example of how being compassionate can lead to burnout.

Give an example of how being responsible can lead to burnout.

Give an example of how being competitive can lead to burnout.

Can you identify another personality trait (maybe one that you have) that could also lead to burnout? Explain.

3. When we forget the way God designed the human body to function (periods of work followed by periods of rest), we put ourselves on a path to almost certain burnout if we only work and fail to rest.

What are the three actions that Pastor Mike says we'll do when we don't pay attention to God's design? (Hint: each word begins with the letter *C*). Describe how these three actions have shown up in your life or experience.

-

-

-

PHYSICAL REST

The first verse of the first chapter of the first book of the Bible says, **"In the beginning God created . . ."** (Genesis 1:1). God created for a period of six days.

The first verse and following of Genesis chapter 2 says, **"Thus the heavens and the earth were completed in all their vast array. By the seventh day God had finished the work he had been doing; so on the seventh day he rested from all his work. Then God blessed the seventh day and made it holy, because on it he rested from all the work of creating that he had done"** (verses 1-3). God created for six days and then rested on day seven.

The Hebrew word for rest is *Shabbat* (you may know this word better as *Sabbath*). It means "to cease," "to stop," or "to rest." The Creator finished his work of creation in six days. Since his creation was perfect and complete, there wasn't anything left to create. So on day seven, he stopped working. He rested. Then he blessed the seventh day and made it holy. In other words, he set the seventh day apart as a special day, a day of rest.

The Creator of the universe instituted—at creation—this weekly rhythm of *Shabbat*. Then at Mt. Sinai several thousand years later, he formalized *Shabbat* for his Old Testament covenant people, the Israelites.

Prior to Sinai, the Israelites had experienced life without *Shabbat*. For about four hundred years, the Israelites lived in Egypt. Some Bible scholars suggest that the Israelites were enslaved by Pharaoh for approximately the last one hundred years that they resided in Egypt. If you were a slave in ancient times, how many vacation days did you get each year? *Zero.* How many PTO days? *Zip.* How much time did you get off each week? *Nada.* As a slave, the only time you weren't working was when you were sleeping. And the only reason slaves needed to sleep was so they could work again the next day. For Pharaoh's slaves, life in Egypt was a life lacking a rhythm of work and rest.

The Lord God called Moses to lead his people out of the slavery of Egypt. Moses went to Pharaoh and asked him to let God's people go out into the desert to worship the Lord. Pharaoh refused Moses' request repeatedly. Each no was followed by a devastating plague sent from the Lord God. Finally, with the tenth plague, which caused the death of every firstborn in Egypt, Pharaoh told Moses and the Israelites to leave.

When the Israelites left Egypt, they headed toward Mt. Sinai. On the way to Mt. Sinai, the Lord God gave his people a concrete way to understand *Shabbat*. When the people complained about having no food, the Lord God provided manna in the morning. The manna was on the ground, and the people gathered it. This happened each morning for six days. But on the seventh day, there was no manna. God directed his people to gather up twice as much manna on day six because there wouldn't be any on the seventh day. The seventh day was to be a day of rest, a day of *Shabbat*.

1. At Mt. Sinai, the Lord God formalized *Shabbat* for his covenant people. Look up the following passages in your Bible and jot down what each passage says about *Shabbat*:

   • Exodus 16:29

   • Exodus 20:10

   • Exodus 23:10,11

   • Exodus 31:14

   • Exodus 31:16

PHYSICAL BURNOUT, PHYSICAL REST

After reading these passages, put in your own words how serious the Lord God was about his covenant people practicing *Shabbat*.

2. In this chapter, Pastor Mike mentioned Jesus' example of practicing *Shabbat* as recorded in Luke 5:15,16:

Crowds of people came. **"But Jesus often withdrew to lonely places and prayed."** *Isn't that fascinating? He worked to love people, and before the work was even done, he withdrew. Some people say you've got to work until the job is done. Jesus said, "Nope." And don't miss the adverb. Jesus withdrew* **"often."** *This wasn't something he did once a year after a crazy time in ministry. He often, by himself and with his disciples, got away. He said, "We've loved these people for a long time; it's time for a break." Jesus' lifestyle and his constant and often habit was to* *withdraw to lonely places just to be with his heavenly Father and rest.*

How does Jesus' rhythm of work and rest compare to the rhythm in your life?

What steps could you take to get into a rhythm more like Jesus'?

3. Also in this chapter, Pastor Mike said:

You don't get to decide if you need sleep or not. That's how God made you. You can learn about food and nutrition, but you don't get to decide what makes you run at peak performance. That's been built into you by the Creator who created the rules. Your body needs exercise whether you decide it does or not. The Creator creates the rules, and God created you with a need to eat and to move and to sleep.

PHYSICAL BURNOUT, PHYSICAL REST

Take a moment and evaluate how well you are doing with the three needs that the Creator built into our bodies—nutritious food, activity/exercise, and sleep. On a scale of 5 to 1 (with 5 being the best), rate yourself. Then list one action you can take that will improve your rating.

NUTRITIOUS FOOD

○ 1   ○ 2   ○ 3   ○ 4   ○ 5

Action to take: _____

_____

_____

ACTIVITY / EXERCISE

○ 1   ○ 2   ○ 3   ○ 4   ○ 5

Action to take: _____

_____

_____

SLEEP

○ 1   ○ 2   ○ 3   ○ 4   ○ 5

Action to take: _____

_____

_____

PRAYER

Dear Lord, thank you so much for the surprising things in your Word that I haven't seen before. In the Old Testament, there's a rhythm of work and rest, of pushing and then pushing pause. I pray that in our culture we could swim a little bit against the tide and not need to grow and progress at the cost of our souls. God, what good is it if I gain the whole world and yet give up my soul or my marriage or the precious time with my children or the body you have given me? I'm praying both for your grace and wisdom. Help me not to live with regret and shame because of the past. Help me to take all that to the cross, and help me make decisions and change my schedule in the way that I need so I can be just like Jesus—full of joy and peace and love. That's a big change for me, God, so I need your help, and I'm so grateful that you're right here to give it to me. Amen.

CHAPTER 2
Spiritual Burnout, Spiritual Rest

If you finished the last chapter with some questions or objections, I don't blame you. We kicked off this book about the Bible and burnout, and we learned the simple truth that the Creator creates the rules. God is the Creator; you and I are part of his creation. Because God is the Creator, he gets to decide the rules for how your body and your mind work—how you emotionally and physically work. God designed you with a need for hard work and movement and also for taking breaks, resting, and sleeping. He designed you with a need for food and drink. You don't get to decide in the morning how your body's going to function; that's already been decided for you. The Creator creates the rules.

You and I live in a modern, digital, American, Christian culture that pushes and pushes for progress and profit and more and better, but we don't get to decide the rules. We compromise and compensate and crash. No, God decides the rules. That's why when Jesus walked the earth two thousand years ago, he followed the rules. He served people, and then he stepped back. He pushed really hard to love people in his Father's name, and then he pushed pause. The Bible says that Jesus often withdrew to be totally by himself, just to be with God, to recharge, and to pray. That's what Jesus did. And that's what God wants you and I to do too.

YOUR OBJECTIONS

But if you read that in the last chapter, you might have a question or an objection. In fact, when I preached on this topic at my church, lots of people asked me questions and gave objections. One business owner said, "Pastor Mike, honestly, my biggest problem is not that I'm working too hard; it's that the people at my business don't work hard enough. I don't want to work 60 or 70 or 80 hours a week, but I can't get, especially some younger people, to work 20 or 25 hours without feeling overwhelmed and exhausted. Isn't the problem not some of us working too much but some people working too little?" Yes, that's also true. It's really great that younger generations are talking about self-care and mental health more than ever before; I affirm that. But sometimes we're so aware of our stress levels that when we get stressed, we never push past it. There are a lot of people—maybe even you—who don't have the traits of endurance and perseverance. You wouldn't survive the boot camp or the farm because your brain's never been developed to push through really difficult things. The Bible says that you should be as tough as a farmer and able to work as hard as a soldier (see 2 Timothy 2:4-6). And if your struggle is with laziness or perseverance, that would be a different book chapter, because that's a very valid objection.

Maybe your objection is more like this: "But, Pastor Mike, aren't there times in life when you have to break the rules? I hear what you're saying. God made my body to need sleep, likely seven to nine hours a night, but I just had a baby seven weeks ago who wakes up every 20 minutes. Aren't there times when the rules get broken? Like final exams if you're a student or tax season if you're an accountant or you're in the medical field and there's a pandemic or you're a pastor and it's Holy Week or you just opened a business about a year ago? Aren't there times when you can't find the time for rest and vacation and working out and sleeping enough?" To that I'd say yes! Read 2 Corinthians chapter 11. The apostle Paul talks about some of the sleepless nights he had as he carried out the gospel. Read about the life of Jesus. Sometimes he got away from the crowds. Sometimes he was harassed by very needy people, and he made time for them. I would say that's valid in our lives too.

There are times and seasons of life when, by God's calling and design, we can't do everything we want to do. But maybe the most important word in that phrase is *seasons*. There are busy seasons of life, but if you're finding that busyness isn't a season like winter is a season, if you're finding that busyness is all your seasons, then God would want to push you a little bit about how hard you're pushing, how much you're doing, how many hours you're investing, and the standards that you have for your daily life.

Maybe your objection is the most common objection. The more I thought about why some of us know the rules and know what we should do with our bodies and yet we break the rules, I kept coming back to this. I have a hunch that if you're exhausted right now and I could counsel you and pull back the layers, I would bet my favorite Bible that at the heart of it is this one objection that almost every human shares. It makes us compromise and push too hard, to sprint instead of running the race God has called us to. Here's the objection: "But, Pastor, I have to do this or someone will be mad. I know you're right. It's too much. I'm too busy. But honestly, I have to do this because if I step back from it, if I take a break, if I slow down, people will not be happy. They won't be proud of me for following the biblical model and Jesus' example. They won't clap. They'll frown. I have to be this busy or someone will be mad."

I have a hunch that's the reason you're running too fast. If you go to your boss tomorrow and say, "Hey, guess what we're learning in church about burnout? I think I've been working too hard, so I'm going to be doing less for the company." Your boss would have some words about that. I doubt he would say, "That's great; good for you. I'm really proud. Go take a nap; take a break if you want." No, if your boss is driven by profit and goals and metrics and investors, he's not going to care about burnout. He's going to care about his thing.

If you're a parent right now who's living in this crazy American sports culture where everyone plays club 58 weekends every year, this is hard. If you say to your son, "Hey, I know all your friends are playing on the team and going to Chicago for the tournament, but our family's just too busy for that. I want to make a homecooked meal and have you at the dinner table." Your competitive son is not going say, "Thanks, Mom. You're such a good person. You're so wise." No, he's going to be furious. He's going to stomp his feet and slam the door and say, "All my friends are going. Why are you the only parent who does this?"

If you cut back, people aren't going to be happy. They're going to be mad, disappointed, and think you're selfish. They're going to wonder why you changed, what's different. They're used to getting this much out of you, and when you dial back to follow the Bible's example, they're not going to clap for you.

I think if I could see your schedule and objectively say things like this: "Well, stop doing this," "You really shouldn't be doing that," "You don't have margin in your schedule for this right now," you'd get emotional and say, "But if I do that, someone will be disappointed."

Honestly, maybe the one who would be disappointed is you. It feels pretty good when people clap. It's really nice to get the Volunteer of the Year award. All of us like to be appreciated and approved of. It's nice not only to make the team but to start. It's not just nice to work there and be an average employee but to be the one whom the boss respects, the one whom he or she can count on. It feels really good when you serve someone and they appreciate it. It feels good. So to step back, to be less than you used to be, even for the sake of your own sanity, it's emotional.

WHAT'S TOO MUCH WEIGHT FOR YOU?

Imagine a barbell with a stack of 5- or 10-pound plates nearby. Imagine one plate represents one of your responsibilities, so you put it on your barbell. And then you have another responsibility, so you put that plate on too. This is enough; you could lift this bar easily. But then someone else wants you to do more, and you agree. So you put on another plate. You think you can volunteer, help out at church, join an extra team, and squeeze in this extra thing—more plates go on the bar. And then someone else wants something from you. You add another plate, thinking you have room for this in your life too. And then someone else wants something from you . . . Phew!

All the small plates put together are too much to carry! So you pull one or two plates off. That feels better. But in real life there's a problem. If you remove a plate, it might feel like a little thing to you, but to the person who gave you the task, it's not a little thing. For example, if the coach wants your kid on the team or in the club so the team can make it to state and if you pull your kid back from that thing, the coach and probably your kid won't be happy.

If your boss has goals and profit margins that he wants to make and you cut back your extra work hours, he might not be happy. He might think he's not asking you to do that much. Just one more shift. Just one more project. But add that to just one more tournament, just one more thing to sign up for at church, and just one more errand to run for your sister, and all those things get really heavy! To your boss it doesn't feel like he is asking you for much because he isn't; he's not trying to be mean or oppressive to you. What he doesn't know is that you're not just carrying his little thing; you're carrying all the things. There's family stuff, friend stuff, life stuff, and neighbor stuff. You might be a parent, a spouse, dating someone, a grandparent, and someone with a main job and a side job. All these things put together—all these 5- and 10-pound plates—add up and leave you exhausted. Maybe you know from experience that if you set something down, if you stop doing something, people will be so disappointed in you.

I think this is the real issue behind the issue. It's a tension that explains so much of our schedules. The answer to your burnout is likely very easy, but for you it is anything but easy. It is emotional because it involves the approval of people. I think the real tension is this: We feel like we have to burn ourselves out or we're going to let someone down.

"I wish there was some easy solution, Pastor, but if I don't do this, someone will be mad. Burn out or let them down. I hate letting people down, so I'm going to choose for another week, another season, another year to push past my Creator's limits."

RESOLVING THE TENSION

The big question is: What are you going to do? You and I live in a culture that will push us in a thousand different ways. It'll encourage us to load up another responsibility, ask us to do more and more and more, and encourage us to make resolutions to do more and more and more. So how will you personally resolve this tension? I want to help you find an answer. We're going to run back to Jesus, because he doesn't just give us the perfect example; he also offers us the perfect solution.

We've already learned that Jesus was okay with disappointing people. We read that crowds of people came to be healed of their sicknesses. They were desperate for Jesus. Can you imagine being someone in line to see him? He heals, he heals, he heals, he heals, and then when it's finally your turn in line, he says, "Sorry, end of my shift." And he walks away with peace and joy in his heart. He's not bad because he knows that God isn't mad; he is honoring the rules of his body. He is okay with people not liking him, being disappointed in him.

Every single day someone was disappointed in Jesus. That's a great example for you. But I want to tell you that Jesus is not just a great example; he offers you the perfect solution. He offers you biblical, divine, and spiritual help at the level of your soul.

Look with me in Matthew chapter 11, which is one of the most beautiful invitations that Jesus ever gave. Jesus says,

SPIRITUAL BURNOUT, SPIRITUAL REST

"Come to me, all you who are weary and burdened, and I will give you rest. Take my yoke upon you and learn from me, for I am gentle and humble in heart, and you will find rest for your souls. For my yoke is easy and my burden is light" (verses 28–30). I love those verses!

First, Jesus says, "Come." It's an invitation. The door's unlocked; it's standing wide open. At the ticket office, there's a ticket that's been paid for with your name on it. Jesus says, "Come to me. Don't come to a place or to some program or some list of things you've got to do like a checklist." Jesus says, "I want to look you in the eye; come to me as a person—all of you. It doesn't matter who you are. It doesn't matter how old you are. It doesn't matter what you've done. It doesn't matter your background, your mistakes, or your sins." Jesus says to you, "Come to me, especially all of you who are weary and burdened. If you've been carrying too much for too long, if you can't keep doing this, if you're impatient and you've lost your joy and fire for God, if you're weary in both body and soul, come to me. I will give you rest. I'm gentle. I'm humble, and I will give you rest for your souls."

Hmm, now *souls* is an interesting little word. You might expect him to say, "Come to me if you're tired out, you're beaten up, or you haven't had a break, and I'll give you rest for your body." But Jesus says, "If you come to me, you will find rest for your *souls*." What does that mean? Apparently Jesus isn't offering you a year's supply of free bath bombs. He won't pay for an all-inclusive trip to a Mexican beach to gorge yourself on the buffet and get away from the stresses of life. No, he brings rest for your soul.

Here's what this means; it's beautiful. What Jesus is saying is at your deepest level—your very soul, your spirit—he wants to offer you the love and approval of God apart from works. Jesus says, "Come to me. I won't give you a long list of things to do. I will give rest to you, gift it to you. You don't work for it. I'm just giving it. And what am I giving you? Rest knowing that God loves you, God likes you, God sees you, and God smiles upon you."

Jesus isn't saying to you, "Come to me, and I'll give you some things you can fix." Or, "Come to me; I'll give you an update on your karma so you can do some good to balance out that bad." He's not saying, "Come to me, and I'll give you a ladder so you can climb your way up to heaven." He's saying, "If you come to me, if you believe in me, I will make you good with God, not by your works but as a pure gift."

I love how the apostle Paul talked about the same concept. In Ephesians chapter 2, Paul said this: **"For it is by grace you have been saved, through faith—and this is not from yourselves, it is the gift of God—not by works, so that no one can boast"** (verses 8,9). How are you saved from God's disappointment, his disapproval, from God being mad or sad or done with you? How are you saved from his wrath, judgment, and condemnation? Paul says, "It is by grace you've been saved." Grace is God's free love. It's not something you work for and can boast about; it's just this gift that Jesus gives to you.

SPIRITUAL BURNOUT, SPIRITUAL REST

Two thousand years ago Jesus lived a flawless, holy life, and he died a perfect, sacrificial death. And Jesus is saying, "If I take away all your sins and leave them at the cross and if I take this perfect life that I lived and put it under your account and if you come to me, God will look at you and smile. He'll see your profile picture and click the little 'thumbs-up.' God will accept you, approve you, love you, like you. He'll delight in you, he'll sing over you, and he'll be proud of you. Not because you've done enough work but because he worked, lived, and died for you."

If you're a longtime Christian, you've heard that message ever since you were a kid growing up in church. But have you ever paused to think about how absolutely beautiful and liberating and unique and wonderful that message is? God likes YOU, even though you haven't done enough work. Let me prove it to you. When you are in school, if you want to make your teacher smile, what do you have to do? Work. If you don't show up for school, if you don't do your homework, if you don't do the presentation, if you flop, your teacher will be disappointed in you. How do you make the teacher smile? You have to work.

When you get older, you get your first job. If you want to make your boss happy, what do you have to do? You have to work. You have to show up and do the stuff and check the boxes and go the extra mile. If you want to make the boss smile, you have to work.

If you are dating or get married and want to make your spouse or significant other happy, what do you have to do?

You have to work. Yeah, if you sit there on the couch and play Call of Duty for your entire marriage, she will not like you very much, right? You have to find out your partner's love language. You have to speak it. You have to serve them. You have to go the extra mile. In every area of life, if you want to see a smile on someone's face, you better work.

But then Jesus comes along and says, "How are you going to make God smile? Help a little old lady across the street? Come on, he's God. You could never do enough works, so how about this. How about I do the work for you. How about I'm perfect for you. How about you come to me if you're tired, at the very level of your soul, and I will give you rest because you can know that today and tomorrow and for all eternity God's going to look at you and his face is going to light up and he's going to see you and he's not going to send you away. He's going to accept you, not with some asterisk but with his arms wide open no matter how deep and messed up your sin is." That's what Jesus offers us. This is the gospel that gives us rest.

So here's the main point. It is the gospel, the good news of what Jesus has done, that gives rest to our souls.

FILL YOUR HEART WITH GOD'S APPROVAL

"But, Pastor, I don't want to interrupt, but I think you just pulled one of those pastor-sermon-Jesus-judo flips on us."

"Well, what do you mean?"

SPIRITUAL BURNOUT, SPIRITUAL REST

"We were talking at the start of this chapter about our schedules, and then you grabbed the Bible and started talking about our salvation. We were talking about disappointing my parents or my kids or my coworkers or my boss; that's why I push too hard. And then you suddenly started talking about Jesus. I see what you did there, Pastor. We were talking about the tension we have to burn out or let someone down, and then you switched to talking about grace and faith and the cross and getting to heaven and making God happy. That's great, and I love the gospel, but you didn't actually fix the tension; you didn't address the problem."

"Good objection."

But I have an answer. We sometimes think the gospel is just a thing for then—a time in the future on the day we die when our sins are gone and God accepts us into heaven. It's true. But the gospel is actually so much more than that. The gospel has benefits for right here and right now that allow us to make the decisions that we need to make.

Let me connect the dots for you. Deep within your heart when God created you, he created a passion to be liked. He did. You could be a pastor, an atheist, young or old, or male or female. All of us, deep down, want someone to see us and smile. Some kids become class clowns because they want to be liked. Maybe you pushed hard to never get a B+ because you wanted to be liked. Maybe you were an amazing athlete or musician because people were impressed and liked you for it. Maybe you had those crazy birthday parties for your kids where you're the mom of the year because of the fancy cake with the Legos on top that your kid loves. We like that. Some of us work hard on sermons because we want people to like us. Some of us work hard on our yards, our sneaker game, our fashion, our filters, our TikTok videos. Why is it that if someone likes your picture or comments something nice about you or compliments you, your heart goes, "Ahhh"? Because God created within you a deep, deep desire for approval and acceptance, to be liked.

But here's the problem: Most of us try to fill that hole in our hearts with the approval of people. We work and work and work to get people to like us. We push and push and push to get people to like us; it feels so good when they do. I don't know if anyone's ever told you this, but if you try to satisfy that craving of your heart with people, it will be both impossible and exhausting. If your goal in life is to feel good because everyone likes you, it's impossible. You can't make everyone happy all the time. And it's exhausting.

My wife feels this all the time. She's super hardworking and super responsible. She'll go the extra mile for these people and these people and these people, and then this person over here still needs her help. "How do I do all of it?" she asks, and she's right. You try to be a great employee, you push hard, and the boss is happy. Then you come home, and you've been an absentee spouse, so your spouse is not happy. It's impossible to make everyone happy. It's exhausting. You push hard, you go the extra mile, you stay late, you come early, you do this for him and her and them, but what about these people? Most of us are trying at the deep level of our souls to find joy and acceptance and peace by making people happy, but it does not work. It kills us.

If you are trying to find your joy in getting people to like you, you will sacrifice some of the most important things that God has given you. If you are trying to get this world to like you and your boss to love you, you will not be a present parent. No, your job will pile you with weight, and you will have nothing left for the people who matter most. If you're trying to get people to like you by doing everything for everyone, you will not take care of your body. It will backfire on you, and people will have to care for you because you haven't cared for yourself. If you're trying to make every coach happy and the scouts happy, you're going to be gone every other weekend. You'll start missing church, and the things of your soul will start to shrivel. When we mess this up and try to fill that space in our hearts with the approval of people, it kills us. It's impossible, and it's exhausting.

That's why Jesus says, "Come to me." Are you weary? Have you been working hard but someone's still disappointed in you? Is it never enough? Are you burdened? All these responsibilities. All these things. It's hard to even sleep. You've got to make sure everything's right in your head. Jesus says, "Come to me, and I will give you rest. I will give you God. I will give you the smile of God. I will give you the applause of angels. I will make you holy so that when all of heaven looks at you, their faces will light up. I will give you so much more than a thumbs-up or a little compliment. I will fill your heart with gallons and gallons of God's grace and acceptance. You have God!"

Why wasn't Jesus a slave to the opinions of people? He had God. He certainly served people; he wanted people to trust in him and follow him, but if the Pharisees were freaking out, did Jesus freak out? They were people. He had God.

Imagine you are dead broke and then get a $20 parking ticket. You freak out because you don't have money for that! If you are Elon Musk with billions in your bank account, you don't care about a $20 ticket. You have plenty of resources; it doesn't bother you. In the same way, if you have no approval, if your heart is just aching when someone doesn't give it to you, you compromise, you push too hard, you burn out. But if you have God, all of God—the bigness and the love of God, the approval of God—if you close your eyes and see your Father in heaven, his face shining upon you and looking on you with favor, well, you don't need people to like you. You hope they do. You're not trying to offend anyone or make them mad, but if they are, well, you're following God.

That reminds me of the story of Bobby Read. Back in 2021, a Florida businessman named Bobby Read wanted to buy a small piece of property that was right next to the city water tower in the town where he lived. So he went to the city, and they drew up the paperwork. He bought this little piece of property for $55,000. And then after the paperwork was signed, both Bobby and the city found out something rather shocking that none of them knew. According to the document, Bobby Read had not just purchased that little piece of land; he had also received the city water tower. He thought he was just getting some land, but he had actually gotten so much more. Don't worry; he gave it back.

Maybe you didn't know this about Christianity. Maybe you thought that when you believed in Jesus, he gave you heaven. You thought you wouldn't go to hell but instead would be in heaven with your loved ones and escape the pain; that's true. Praise God. But the gospel gives you so much more. Because of what Jesus has done, right now you get the love of God, the presence of God, the double thumbs-up approval of God, a God whose face is shining on you right now, not just in the future. You could spend your whole life burning out and trying to make everyone happy, or you could listen to this: "Come to me all of you who are weary and burdened, and you will find rest for your souls."

HOW TO CHANGE YOUR SCHEDULE

One answer to burnout that so many Christians miss is this: Schedule with the gospel. When you make your schedule, when you have this much work and this much rest, when you say yes to these things and these people and no to those things and those people, schedule with the gospel. That way when someone is mad or disappointed, when you're not getting the approval and praise that you used to, you don't need it. Through the gospel you have God, and God is enough.

What would it look like this year to schedule with the

gospel? If you're tired and burdened, if you're weary, if you're doing too much, if you're not sleeping, if you're not working out, if you don't have downtime for you and your loved ones to relax and just be, if you're not like Jesus, what would you change? What would you step back from? To whom would you say, "You know, it's been an honor to serve, but I'm going to need to be a little bit different this year"? What hard conversations would you have to have? Someone might be disappointed, but after it's over, you could breathe and find rest.

As you think of that, let me tell you what I do. Many years ago, I got some brilliant advice that led me to the conclusion for what's best for me, my soul, my marriage, my kids, and my ministry. I work about 50 hours a week: six eight- to nine-hour days and one day of rest. That feels very biblical, and for 15 years, that's what I've done. I try to push hard so I'm not lazy. I'm not walking. I'm here to serve my church. I work from Sunday to Friday to serve in Jesus' name, but then on Fridays at about 5:00 P.M., things change. Friday is date night. If you ask me to meet on Friday, I will ask you, "Are you dying?" If you say, "No," I'll say, "Sorry, it's date night." And if you say, "Yes," I'll say, "Call one of the other pastors." No. I won't say that. ☺ There are exceptions and seasons when you need to serve people. But my marriage thrives when week after week after week, Kim and I have time to look each other in the eyes and catch up, take a walk, eat good food, do all the things. It's nonnegotiable for me.

Saturday is the one day I get to wear stretchy pants. I don't shave or use hair product. The day is for my family, my kids. They say, "Dad, do you want to . . . ?" Or, "What else are we going to do?" We clear out the schedule. The day is for rest and allowing us to be together. We cook good food together and go on walks together. That's nonnegotiable for me.

On Sunday when people say that they plan to be at church and ask me to meet, I tell them, "No." That's because I've got to give my best to my church. The most important thing I do that day is preach with a sharp mind and an active body.

People ask me to play soccer all the time; I love playing soccer. But it's one night a week, not two. You say you really need someone to sub, but that's not my jam. I'm sorry if you're disappointed, but if I say yes to you, I say no to my kids and family dinner. I've learned over the years that every time I say yes to a speaking engagement or an extra this or that, I'm saying no to many other things, many of which I really deeply love.

It's hard at first, but you build up the muscle of disappointing people. Many times they aren't as disappointed as you assume. You get into these beautiful rhythms where you look at your sleep schedule, and it's healthy. And you look at how much you've worked out, and it's healthy. And you think of how many times you're around the dinner table instead of the drive-through, and it feels right. Some of you might love that and respect that. Some of you might be disappointed that I'm not working hard enough, but I'm okay if you're disappointed. Years ago, I heard a pastor's wife say, "In life you will always disappoint someone. Don't let it be your kids." So if I'm a mediocre pastor and a great dad, I will not die with regret.

BEYOND BURNOUT

How about you? As you think about what matters most—your soul, your body, your family—what can you say yes to and what can you say no to? I don't know what your schedule will look like, but I do know this: Whether people respect it or hate it, whether they approve of it or shake their heads at it, it really doesn't matter when you schedule with the gospel—remembering that you already have the approval of God because of what Jesus did for you. That's the good news of Jesus, who said, "Come to me, all you who are weary and burdened, and I will give you rest."

SPIRITUAL BURNOUT, SPIRITUAL REST

DIGGING DEEPER

SPIRITUAL BURNOUT

1. In this chapter, Pastor Mike said:

   > I think this is the real issue behind the issue. It's a tension that explains so much of our schedules. The answer to your burnout is likely very easy, but for you it is anything but easy.... I think the real tension is this...

   What is the tension that Pastor Mike identified?

   Give one or two examples of how this tension has shown up in your life or experience.

2. To address this tension, Pastor Mike encouraged us to turn to Jesus' words in Matthew chapter 11:

   "**Come to me, all you who are weary and burdened, and I will give you rest. Take my yoke upon you and learn from me, for I am gentle and humble in heart, and you will find rest for your souls. For my yoke is easy and my burden is light.**" (verses 28-30)

   What is the significance of Jesus saying, "Come to me"?

   List the top three issues in your life today that make you weary and burdened.

What kind of rest is Jesus inviting you to receive from him?

What is it that actually gives rest to your soul? Explain what that looks like in your life or experience.

3. What does "schedule your life with the gospel" mean for you? How will your life look different when you schedule your life with the gospel?

BEYOND BURNOUT

SPIRITUAL REST

Nine times in the gospel of Mark, we see Jesus going on a spiritual retreat either by himself or with his disciples. It was part of the rhythm in his life and ministry. Jesus modeled for his followers (and us!) what he encouraged his followers to do in Matthew 11:28-30.

Look up in your Bible the nine spiritual retreats listed below.

- Read the verses.
- Describe in detail what Jesus did during the retreat.
- Consider what happened right before the retreat and right after, noting if there is anything significant.
- Write down a personal takeaway, something you want for your own life.

Mark 1:9-13

SPIRITUAL BURNOUT, SPIRITUAL REST

Mark 1:35

Mark 1:45

Mark 3:13 (Luke 6:12,13 gives additional detail)

Mark 6:30-32

SPIRITUAL BURNOUT, SPIRITUAL REST

Mark 6:45,46

Mark 9:2-13

Mark 14:12-31

Mark 14:32-42

PRAYER

Father, it's tricky because I can't see your face, but I can see theirs. I can't hear the angels applauding when I make wise decisions, but I can read people's comments and their texts. So I really need your help today, as the Bible says, to walk by faith and not by sight. Open the eyes of my heart to see you by faith, to know that if your face is shining upon me today, I have everything I need. I have you. If the Lord is my Shepherd, I shall not want anything. I shall not be in need. I will have learned the secret of being content and the secret of being balanced and not burned out.

Father, there are a lot of people who are used to pleasing people. They're used to being the people who are always there to step up and step in. There are some people who are used to excelling and exceeding and impressing. For all of us who are like that, God, we need you today to remind us that what we have in Christ is so much bigger and so much better. I thank you today for Jesus' love. I thank you today for the gift of heaven, which I will receive one day. And I thank you also for the gift of God's approval, which I receive on this day by faith. In Jesus' name. Amen.

CHAPTER 3

Emotional Burnout, Emotional Rest

You can learn a lot about life from a piece of notebook paper, especially those two thin red lines that run from top to bottom about an inch from the very left side of the page. Those lines create a space that we call the margin. If my research is correct, the purpose of a margin on a piece of paper was originally for mice. I didn't know that. Apparently back in the day, mice would sneak into offices looking for snacks. They found the very edges of paper very tasty, so they nibbled away, and a person could lose the first inch of a sentence they had written. Some genius said, "Let's not let that happen again," and they created a margin.

Yet even today, though mice aren't a problem like they used to be to the same extent, we've retained those two little red lines and the space for different purposes. We have margins on pieces of paper for a bunch of different reasons. For example, maybe what you write in the bulk of the paper is good, but it's not great. Later you think of something really good that you didn't say when you sat down to write originally. A margin gives you space to add notes for something better. Or say you share your work with someone and they see a place for improvement, a chance to make something great absolutely excellent. If there's no space on the page, they can't add that suggestion or improvement. If you have a margin, they can.

Margins are pleasing to the eye too. Can you imagine reading a book if the words went from edge to edge and top to bottom with no space? Have you ever seen a letter where someone actually did that on a piece of paper? When you saw that, did you wonder if the person was okay or if you should call someone for help? It's unsettling, and it's stressful. Margins, blank spaces, are actually a gift in so many ways.

In the previous chapters of this book, I've essentially been talking about the good work that God wants to write into our lives and the margins he wants to bless us with. We've seen that our heavenly Father created us in a way that allows us to work hard and serve people, but then there should be space to Sabbath and breathe and rest. It's actually the way that Jesus himself lived. He loved people sacrificially and selflessly like no other human being who has ever lived, but not constantly. Instead, we saw in the gospel of Luke that Jesus often withdrew to lonely places, not to do stuff for people but to be with the most important person, his heavenly Father.

We also saw that Jesus isn't just a great example; he is the greatest blessing. He gives us the most important thing that our hearts need: the love of God and the acceptance of God and the approval of God. Not because we've worked so hard and done so much but as a free gift through his life, his death on a cross, and his resurrection. Jesus invites us: "Come to me if you're weary and tired and burdened and burned out, and I will give you rest for your soul."

God wants you to work hard and love people, but not 24/7. Your heavenly Father created you for work and rest, for service and Sabbath.

MARGINS ARE IMPORTANT!

Can I confess something to you? Whenever I sit down to write a sermon, I open up a document on my MacBook Pro, and the very first thing I do every single time is minimize the margins. The standard form says one inch on the left, one inch on the top, one inch on the right, and one inch on the bottom. But the very first thing I do is click the margins down to the lowest they'll let me go. I do this because I want to put a full sermon—30 to 40 minutes, 2,000 to 3,000 words in Times New Roman 10-point font—on a single piece of paper. You might see it and say, "Is he okay? Should I call someone?"

But once I have it on one sheet of paper, I run into a problem when I'm practicing the sermon with this first draft. I think, "No, that doesn't work; that doesn't flow. Ooh, I thought of this other idea, but there's no space to put it." I can't write my ideas down because there aren't any margins. See the problem? Enough about me. Let's talk about you.

If last week was a piece of paper or last year could fit onto a page, how much margin was there for you? Maybe for you the answer is a lot; maybe the answer is too much. You had time to binge every season of your favorite show in less than a month. You had a lot of margin. You scrolled TikTok or Instagram every day. You haven't worked a 50-hour week in forever. That could be you. Maybe your struggle is that you need to run more, not walk the race God has called you to.

But I would bet in our culture today, for every one person who struggles with laziness, there are probably five who struggle with burnout. These are people who minimize the margins, who squeeze in an extra commitment, who push the hours and compromise the rules that God has set up for their bodies. Are you one of those people? If someone could see your day planner or watch you on a reality show to see your schedule, would they react in the same way some of you would react to my marginless sermon: "Oh, does he need help? Should I say something?" It's unsettling when you see a page filled up from edge to edge, and it's very unsettling when you see a life filled up from start to finish.

Here's what I think might be happening to you. Even though you've read this far in this book, even though I can prove to you from the Bible that Jesus rested, even though Sabbath is a huge theme throughout the Scriptures, even though your heart has everything it needs in Jesus, even though the Father created you with rules to sleep and unplug and rest and not serve people all the time, you maybe haven't changed a thing just yet. You have the same commitments, same craziness, same pace, and same pushing it. What if you and I were in a quiet office with cups of coffee and I asked you, "Why are you doing this again? Last year's page was to the edge; it seems like you're repeating it for round two. Why are you doing that again?" In that vulnerable moment, I bet you would repeat to me some things that you believe deep down at an emotional level that make it almost impossible for you to slow down and stop. I would say there are lies or half-truths that you believe in your head. They're very important to your heart, and no matter what I say or what passage I quote, you won't slow down because you think you can't slow down.

THREE LIES WE BELIEVE

There's a whole list of lies people believe that keep them busy. I want to share just three of them with you. I think they lead to frequent burnout.

Lie number one: It has to be perfect. Maybe you're someone who does good work, gets good grades, and your boss thinks you're a good employee, but for you, good just isn't good enough. It has to be perfect. Maybe your parents said this to you: "You're still studying? You're doing fine. Your teachers love you. You get good grades." But for some, an

88 is absolutely unacceptable, as is a 92 or a 94 or 96 or 97. They have a reputation for a super high level of academic excellence. The world would be fine. They would still make it to heaven if they got a B, but they can't get a B. It has to be perfect.

Some people are that way at work. They put together a presentation or a pitch; the numbers are strong. There's no chance they will get fired. They've been faithful to their job, but faithful just isn't good enough. They have to be perfect, so they rewrite the email and improve the project and stay up late with the laptop open in bed. They don't just want to be good at their job but great at it, perfect at it.

For some, this happens on social media. They have to keep a perfect Snapchat streak with friends or they will "die." Some have to pick the perfect filter, have to update the post; it can't just be okay or good. It has to be perfect.

For some, this is true when it comes to how they look. They've got to try on another dress or shirt. They've got to put on just the right outfit. Which shoes match? What looks best? Next they work on their hair or makeup. It can take literally an hour every single day because they don't want to look fine or average; they want to look as good as they possibly can. They want to look perfect.

In a thousand different ways—our education, our athletics, not just making the team but starting, not just starting but being all-conference—we're busy and exhausted and really don't have the time, but we push it. Here's why. It's very, very emotional and important for us to be perfect.

EMOTIONAL BURNOUT, EMOTIONAL REST

Or how about lie number two. *Lie number two is that we have to make everyone happy.* I covered this in the last chapter at a deeper level, but it is such a pervasive thought. It's so personal to so many that I want to cover it again briefly. If peace and joy and resting in Jesus didn't define your last year because you were "busy" all year long, when you flip the calendar and do the same things again, how will anything be different? If I say, "Isn't that the definition of insanity? What do you think is going to happen to you this year?" The answer is: the same thing that happened last year! You're going to miss all the promises and goodness and peace of Jesus because you'll be running, running, running. You'll be exhausted.

My wife and I run together. If we try to sprint side by side, the conversation is not great. We have to slow down to a pace that's not perfect for running but good for talking and connecting. I might ask you, "Why aren't you slowing down so you can connect with Jesus?"

You might say, "Well, if I change this, that person won't be happy. If I stop volunteering, if I don't coach my kids, if I tell my boss I can't do as much, if I step back from what people are used to receiving from me, if I don't host the holiday party again, if I don't make the famous dessert that everyone loves to eat, people will not be happy. They'll be sad or mad." And instead of saying, "Okay, well that's how they feel," you feel very responsible for other people's emotions, which is a destructive way to live. Instead of saying, "Okay, he's mad," you panic and say, "He's mad! And I have to fix that!" No, you don't. "She's disappointed in me. Obviously, I need to work harder." Nope, nope, nope. She's disappointed, sure. Period.

For some people, that deep desire to have everyone like them and love them and applaud them and approve of them means they can never slow down. They will say yes to everything everyone asks them to do, and there will be no exit ramp until they crash and burn, because deep down they believe they have to make everyone happy.

Or how about lie number three: *"It's fine."* Also known as, "I'm fine." Also known as, "Whatever."

"How many weekends was your family gone to sports tournaments?"

"Yeah, it's crazy, but it's fine."

"How many hours do you sleep? How much coffee do you drink?"

"Yeah, I know, but I'm fine."

Some think deep down in their hearts that God has given them a cheat code. Back when I was growing up playing the original Nintendo, there was a game called Contra. If you played Contra and knew the cheat code—up, down, up, down, left, right, left, right, A, B, select, start—you'd get unlimited lives. You could do whatever you wanted. You could jump off a cliff or get shot by the enemy because you were fine, whatever. Some people think they have a cheat code to life.

"I go through the drive-through. I go through the drive-through. I go through the drive-through. I skipped a workout. I skipped a workout. I work too much. I work too much. I never slow down. I never slow down. It's fine." But God didn't make us for that.

"My doctor is appalled by my lifestyle. Kind of funny, isn't it?" No. But if you believe that—that you're the exception to the Creator's rules, that just because nothing has happened yet means nothing will happen—you won't change.

So whether you're striving for perfection, trying to make everyone in your life happy, or just thinking that you're the exception to God's rules, all of us have some lie or lies that keep us sprinting instead of running the race that God has called us to.

So I want to grab the Bible, the Word of God, and take those lies head-on. I want to push them out of your brain, convince you with the help of the Holy Spirit, and replace them with God's truth so you can shake free from the slavery of needing to be perfect and to make everyone happy or the foolishness of thinking it's fine. That's the goal. Replace those three lies with three bits of God's truth, not so you walk in laziness but so you slow down and not sprint in foolishness. Instead, run the race that Jesus has called you to.

BEATING LIE NUMBER ONE

Lie number one: It has to be perfect. I want to share with you what the apostle Paul wrote in 1 Corinthians chapter

4, a time in his life when he was under severe criticism for not being good enough at something. Did you know that the apostle Paul was critiqued and criticized for not being good enough at public speaking? Shocking, huh? He started a church in the Greek city of Corinth. Apparently, Paul admitted that he wasn't as good at this kind of stuff as other people. And after he left to start other churches, people came in and critiqued him: "Paul's a chump. Paul wouldn't get enough YouTube views; he's not good enough." They criticized him and critiqued him. He wasn't perfect at that craft. To defend himself and the validity of his ministry, Paul responded with these words from 1 Corinthians chapter 4: **"This, then, is how you ought to regard us: as servants of Christ and as those entrusted with the mysteries God has revealed. Now it is required that those who have been given a trust must prove faithful"** (verses 1,2).

Paul didn't panic that he wasn't perfect at public speaking. He said, "No, I'm certain that Jesus entrusted this ministry to me. Yes, I preach, but when God evaluates me as a preacher, he's not going to say, 'Were you perfect? Did you put any *ums* or *ahs* in your sentences? Could you move people to tears, Paul? Could you tell the right story to get them at the end?' No. It is required of me as one who's been given a trust that I must prove in the eyes of God to be faithful."

Here's my application for you. Let's think about the things that God has entrusted to your life. Maybe you have not been entrusted with a call to be a missionary or to preach the gospel from a stage, but I bet God has entrusted you with some very important things. How about a physical body? God's given you a body. He has some things to say about it: Be faithful to the body he's given you. Work and rest, sleep and exercise, get good nutrition.

God's entrusted you with a soul. Souls need to be cared for with the Word of God, grace, and truth.

Have you been entrusted with a spouse? That's a sacred trust, to love as Christ has first loved you.

Have you have been entrusted with children? That's a sacred trust too.

Are your parents still living? Honoring and loving your parents is a trust too.

Here's what really wise people know that perfectionists forget. If you've been entrusted with a handful of things and try to be perfect in one of them, you probably will not be faithful with the rest of them. I think that's probably the most important thing I'm going to write in this chapter, so let me write it again. If you try to be perfect in one of the things that God has entrusted to you, you will run out of time and energy to be faithful with all the things that God has entrusted to you.

Maybe you actually grew up this way. Maybe you don't have a super close relationship with your dad, but your dad had a super close relationship with his work. He strove to be perfect. He put in extra hours. The boss loved him. He accomplished great things. There's nothing wrong with doing good work. The problem for your dad was that he strove for perfection in the work area of his life, and as a limited human being only, he had so much time and so much energy. When he came home, was he faithful to the things God had entrusted to his care? Was he faithful to you? That's the dark side of perfection.

This sometimes happens to parents. We want to be perfect parents. We want our kids to have the best lives. We want them to be involved in all the things, so we sign them up for this and that and those lessons and these tournaments and those opportunities. We pour ourselves in. We sit on bleachers every single weekend. We try to be perfect parents, but what happens if we try to be perfect parents? I've seen this too often; we're often very unfaithful spouses. Or we're exhausted from all the kid stuff. Is there time and energy for us to love like Christ loves his bride? Do we have ways to show respect and speak each other's love languages, or have the kids absolutely exhausted us of everything? If we try to be perfect in one thing, we end up very unfaithful in another. In so many different ways, as limited human beings, if we overextend ourselves in A, we're not going to be faithful at B and C and D.

Here's what scriptural, wise believers do: They say no to most things. They focus on the few things that God has entrusted to their care. And they know they're never going to be the best at any of these. Will there be better public speakers than me, for example? Millions of them. Will there be better husbands than me? Not to my wife, Kim, but yes. Will there be better fathers than me? For sure. Will there be better athletes than me? Yes, and I'm okay with that because to be perfect, to strive for it in any of those areas, would cost me something that matters way too much: my body, my soul, my relationships, my work. Paul said if God has given you a trust, it is required that you should prove yourself faithful.

So in the name of Jesus, I give you permission to be average at stuff. The only other option is to look back on life with regret. When I get much older, I want to have a close relationship with my grown daughters. That means I have to make some choices now so they want to be close with me when they're grown. Don't be perfect; it costs too much. Be faithful.

I have one last bit of advice. Be careful of social media. On social media, you see people's perfection, but there's no algorithm that rates their faithfulness. You might see a guy who's really ripped at the gym with a woman who looks amazing in her swimsuit. What you don't know is the state of their souls. Has she neglected her most important relationships? Has he? You might see a post of the traveling team with their championship trophy. But do you know if the members of the team have been faithful to all their callings? You see one thing that's going great, but you don't see the four things that are falling apart. So take it with a grain of salt. Most posts are people's perfection, not their faithfulness. Find someone up close who is faithful, who says no more than they say yes, whose life is balanced and biblical, and imitate them. God doesn't want you to strive for perfection in one calling but to be faithful in all of them.

BEATING LIE NUMBER TWO

"I have to make everyone happy." The apostle Paul addressed this lie as well. Here's what he said: **"I care very little if I am judged by you or by any human court; indeed, I do not even judge myself. My conscience is clear, but that does not make me innocent. It is the Lord who judges me"** (1 Corinthians 4:3,4).

Wow. Isn't that an amazing Scripture? These days we're kind of used to the idea of not caring if someone judges us. What did Taylor Swift say? Haters are gonna hate; you need to shake them off and ignore that stuff. But Paul said something that is so unlike Taylor Swift and everyone else in America. He said, "Indeed, I don't even judge myself. What do I think? I don't care. Do I think I'm a good person? Is this my truth?" Paul said, "No. You don't get to judge me; I don't even get to judge me. I'm trying to do what's right; my conscience is clear. But that doesn't make me innocent." Here's his point: "It is the Lord who judges me. I'm not trying to make me happy. I'm not trying to make you happy. I'm trying to make God happy."

That truth is so liberating and so beautiful. I want to make God happy. When I get to the end of every day, my goal is not to think, "Did I do the things I wanted? Is everyone speaking well of me?" The number-one, most liberating question is, "Is God happy? Is there a smile on God's face?" Here's the gospel. If you are connected to Jesus through faith, yes, there's a smile on God's face. I love this about the

EMOTIONAL BURNOUT, EMOTIONAL REST

Christian faith; it's not a list of things to do. It's a reminder of what Jesus has done. Everything about you that would make God unhappy was removed by Jesus, and he left it at his cross. Anything that would make God scowl instead of smile, he highlighted with his cursor. And when he shed his blood, he pushed delete. If you're a follower of Jesus, every single day you wake up to God's happy face. You fall asleep to it, and you get it all day. His face shines upon you. It looks on you with favor.

It's great if other people like you and me, but we don't need them to like us because God himself likes us. I love it when people click the little thumbs-up button on my posts, but I don't need that to be happy. God, through his Son, gives you and me the thumbs-up. We have the most amazing gifts in the world: the smile of God, his presence, and his love.

And if that weren't enough, when we follow God faithfully, when we do things whether people get it or not, some Christians say that's a God-pleasing decision. Have you heard that phrase before? To live a God-pleasing life? If you set down something that's too much for you this year and people aren't pleased, you need to ask yourself, "Does it make God happy?" Maybe you decide to minimize the margins of your schedule and say no to some things that you said yes to last year, and people say, "Why are you stepping back?" Close your eyes and see the face of God who says, "Yes, I like that. Work and rest. Serving and then stepping back; that makes me happy."

We sometimes think, especially in the church world,

that the only stuff that makes God happy is going to church, volunteering, and coming to events, but that's not true. Those things make God happy, and so do sleeping and resting and recharging. It wasn't like the heavenly Father looked at Jesus when he was in the crowds and said, "Yes!" And then when Jesus got on the boat to get away, "No." All of it was God-pleasing! And when you think the only stuff that makes God happy is when you're doing, doing, doing, you've missed about half of what the Bible has to say. The Creator who created the rules for your body is pleased when you take time to make something healthy. Whether you're on your knees by your bed praying or at the gym lifting, both of those things are pleasing to the Lord. So I want you to see, in a very big and holistic way, all of this makes God happy.

I've told some of the people at my church this story maybe four times now. I'm sorry if you've heard or read it before, but it's probably the best advice I've gotten in my whole life. It has protected me from burnout in the 15 years that I've been a pastor. It has blessed my marriage, my children, my body, and my soul.

When I was around 26, I was about to become a pastor for the very first time. My home pastor in Green Bay, Wisconsin, said, "Mike, whatever church you end up at, wherever you get called to, I want you to go to your very first leadership meeting and I want you to ask the leaders of your church how many hours you should work."

And I said, "No. No, I'm not going to do that. That sounds like terrible advice! You know, 'What's the minimum I have

EMOTIONAL BURNOUT, EMOTIONAL REST

to put in around here so you don't fire me or get really angry?'"

And my pastor said, "No, no, no. You don't get it. You could work 60, 70, 80 hours a week, and then you wouldn't be at one thing and someone would be mad at you. So ask them what it looks like to be faithful as a pastor."

So I did. Short version: I said: "I want to run and not sprint and crash. I don't want to be another pastor who's amazing until he morally fails because he's running on fumes. I don't want to be the guy whom you love as a church but whose wife and children don't love because he's always at church. I don't want to preach out of an empty soul but times of refreshment that I've had in the Word of God. Not because I'm trying to double-duty it, studying for a sermon and calling it my personal devotion. I want to serve you well for a long time." And I asked the people in that room, "How many hours could you do that?" And they gave me answers.

One guy said, "Oh, 45." Another said, "55." Someone said, "I could work 50." Another said, "50." Another said, "50." One said, "60." One said, "40." So we took the average of all the numbers and came up with a faithful workweek: 50 hours. Not scrolling Facebook but serving people in God's Word. And now for 15 years, that's exactly what I've done. I've tried to work hard and be faithful, but I've been able to step away. Before I had a number, I would always feel guilty. I could be doing more. The sermon could be better. Someone needs my help. A guest came to church; I could follow up. The work was never-ending, so I needed a place not to feel bad when I stopped, to know that God was still smiling and I was being faithful.

I know your work is different than mine, but it's really important for you to know where the line is of how much you can invest. When you get to the other side of it, God's not scowling. If you work hard to serve people in love and then you step away, it doesn't make you bad or unfaithful or unlike Jesus. Actually, it makes you just like Jesus, who for every second of his life made his heavenly Father happy.

BEATING LIE NUMBER THREE

Last but not least, lie number three: "It's fine. I'm fine." The tricky thing about that lie is you're probably right . . . right now. It's not like if you sleep four hours a night, drink four cups of coffee in the morning, and skip your workouts this week that you will die by next Monday. It's kind of the tricky thing about seeds and fruit. You don't see what they become or what they don't today or tomorrow; it takes a bit. But for a person who's breaking the rules that the Creator put into their body, it's playing with fire. It catches up to them. Maybe you've been living physically and with your schedule kind of like that person who never wears their seatbelt in the car. They're always texting and driving. "It's fine; dumb rules. I don't need them. Nothing's happened."

To which I would say, "Yet."

But if you who aren't a reader and you're not going to

binge ten books on burnout, let me tell you what I learned when I binged them. Every big story of burnout has the exact same script: Talented, accomplished person who did well at their job had extra opportunities because they were good at their job. They said yes to those opportunities and ran out of time for rest and Sabbath and sleep. They got more opportunities because they worked more hours, until it got to the point where it stopped being fun and peaceful and joyful and felt like an obligation, an obligation that they carried until they compromised, until their bodies—boom—blew up.

I read a book by a doctor who said she was stunned when she needed medication for her depression because during her whole career, she had just given it to other people who were depressed. Her burnout caused depression. Or the amazing pastor from Canada who was respected as a Christian leader in the ministry who thought he could cheat God's rules, but he could not. When he blew up and doubted his own faith and stopped being able to sense the presence of God or believe God's promises, the pastor realized he was not fine. He needed to restart and follow the simple things that we've been learning.

Maybe you haven't blown up your life yet. *Yet.* And that is only because of the absolute mercy and patience of God. You've been working way too much, striving for perfection way too often, neglecting the one and only body that God has given you, and nothing's happened yet. If so, thank the Lord Jesus it's not too late. But before you go crashing into that burnout wall at 80 miles an hour, God's giving you a chance today to pump the breaks, slow down, and drive the car of life at a pace that he designed you to drive.

Maybe you need to hear this passage from Proverbs chapter 1. It says, **"The complacency of fools will destroy them** (to be complacent, to not change)**; but whoever listens to me** (to the voice of wisdom) **will live in safety"** (verses 32,33). Maybe you're pushing it. All last year, all your life, you've been pushing it. If you're complacent after learning these truths from God's Word and think it's fine, here's the promise: It will destroy you. It will catch up to you. Something will fall apart. But it doesn't have to be that way. Whoever listens to the voice of wisdom, the Word of God, will live in safety.

Here's the truth I want to put into your head today. Wise people change before they crash. Today is your opportunity to change. Maybe to disappoint your own standards, to disappoint other people, and to save yourself from something that is 6 months, 12 months, 2 years down the road. It could be a burnout you deeply regret and wish you could come back to this day and say, "Why? Why didn't I listen?" You can listen. "Whoever listens to me will live in safety," God says.

Let me summarize it this way: For the past three chapters, God the Father; his Son, Jesus; and the Holy Spirit have been sitting here, invisibly reaching out compassionate arms to you. The Father, your Creator, says, "I made you. I was there. I knit you together in your mother's womb. I love you; I know how your body works. Listen to me."

Then Jesus says, "Amen, Dad." He says, "Come to me,

and I'll give you rest. If you're running just because you want love and approval in your heart, I'm giving it to you for free. I lived and died for you so a smile would always be on God's face."

The Holy Spirit says, "Amen and amen! Let me fill you with wisdom. Let me renew your mind with the Word of God so you don't believe these lies that will make you lose way too much."

Father, Son, Holy Spirit—can you see their three faces? Their arms extend to you, and they say, "We love you. We want what's best for you. We want to bless you and not watch you burnout. Listen to us."

My wife and I are trying to listen. Kim is like a classic German Protestant. She's reliable, dependable, hardworking. You put a ball in Kim's hands, and she will not drop it. She does what she says she'll do, and she's a woman of incredible character. She pushes; she's an amazing woman to have as a wife. She has a checklist for her checklist, and there's a backup checklist just in case she loses the first checklist for the other checklist. That's Kim.

Then in 1999, she met me. I'm a box checker myself. I love to succeed, try new things, swing for the fences, do things that are big and grand and wonderful and really impressive. So the box-checking, work hard, nose-to-the-grindstone woman met the high-achieving man. We got married, and what could go wrong? Well, nothing at first. I went to grad school and worked three jobs. She started as a preschool and kindergarten teacher, which were some long hours. But there was enough to fit in, and there was a little bit of margin for us to date and workout. But then we had a baby. I love my kids more than anything but, wow, that was a game changer. The new baby was an energy and time vacuum. Oh, what happened to life?! Things became really hard. Then 15 months later, whoops, baby number two. To be candid with you, it wasn't funny because it almost broke us. We weren't unfaithful sexually in marriage, but we were just not faithful to the vows we had made. We poured out everything into work and into the kids, and we weren't connected as a couple. We actually went to counseling to get help with that.

By the grace of God, my parents moved into our basement. They helped us raise those two kids and made it possible for me to work and Kim to work. Next we moved to Appleton, and there wasn't a lot of margin, but there was some. What happened to us is what some people have called the squeeze years. Have you ever heard of them? Our kids are now teens. They're involved, they have friendships, and they need rides. One is in high school, wants to go to the basketball games, and wants to stay connected. There's piano lessons and drum lessons and musical practice and volleyball and club volleyball and tournaments.

Then we have our parents who are very local and very close to us. As they get into their 70s, they can't do what they used to do. They need help with yardwork and technology and passwords and codes and all the updates. There's stuff with the kids that's getting busier. There's stuff with our parents that's getting busier, and to honor your parents does not only mean not to talk back to them when you're 17. It means to love and serve them as their bodies slow down.

Our margins went from an inch, to three-quarters, to a half, to a quarter. We feel it. I'm not asking for your pity; it's a first world problem. But my wife does not push hard from 9 to 5; she pushes hard from 5 to 9. Actually, 4:00 A.M. is when she wakes up to get to the gym and read her Bible before she crashes hard at 8:42 P.M. This season of life and this book are very personal to us. We've gotten all the things done. The balls are still in the air that we were juggling, but it's hard to rejoice in Jesus when you're sprinting too much. So recently we made a huge decision. My wife, who probably works 50 to 60 hours a week as a preschool teacher during the school year, said I can't do that and this and the kids and the us. So we made the massive choice to move her from a full-time teaching job to 20 hours a week. If I told you that wasn't emotional, I'd be straight up lying to you. We thought about the little kids who just love Ms. Kim. We thought about the parents who send her the sweetest notes: "What a blessing that you taught my kid about Jesus." We thought about the great needs of our church's ministry, which is growing. We need more people to serve, not less. We felt the pressure of disappointing people and making them unhappy. It's the kingdom of God! We're working for Jesus; it's our job! We're stepping back?

My wife and I have been learning about the things I'm writing here in this book. They matter, because we don't want to be perfect in one area and unfaithful in others. We've taken a step, and we're not looking back. We know when we close our eyes that God's not disappointed in us; he's actually very happy.

How about you? You probably have an emotional choice to make too. You'll feel the tension of so many good things at the same time. But I tell you this: as hard as it is in the moment, a year from now you will not regret it.

Kim and I try to run together most Saturday mornings. Some days the wind is blowing pretty strong. We get to the end of the driveway and choose to turn into the wind or run with it. It's really tempting to run with the wind, but after you run three miles, do you know what happens? You've got to run home. Or call Uber; I never thought of that. . . . So she and I have this phrase that's our philosophy of life: *into the wind*. Let's do the hard thing right now because there's going to come a time when we can turn around, and life will be so much more enjoyable.

Would you go into the wind, do the hard thing, make the hard decisions? It will not be easy; it will not be unemotional, but you will get to that moment when you'll turn around, feel the wind of God's blessing at your back, and find the very thing that Jesus promised: rest.

DIGGING DEEPER

EMOTIONAL BURNOUT

1. In this chapter, Pastor Mike identifies the three biggest lies that lead to frequent burnout. What are the three lies?

   Lie #1:

   Lie #2:

   Lie #3:

2. Describe how each of these lies has shown up (or is currently showing up) in your life or experience.

   Lie #1:

   Lie #2:

   Lie #3:

In the Old Testament, there was a prophet by the name of Elijah who suffered from emotional burnout. His pain was so great that he even prayed that he might die:

> **Elijah was afraid and ran for his life. When he came to Beersheba in Judah, he left his servant there, while he himself went a day's journey into the wilderness. He came to a broom bush, sat down under it and prayed that he might die. "I have had enough, Lord," he said. "Take my life; I am no better than my ancestors." (1 Kings 19:3,4)**

3. Read 1 Kings 18:16-46. What emotional high would Elijah have experienced because of what happened on Mt. Carmel? Explain.

4. Read 1 Kings 19:1,2. What emotional low would Elijah have experienced because of the words and actions of Queen Jezebel? Explain.

5. Read 1 Kings 19:5-9. Describe how the angel of the Lord addressed Elijah's emotional burnout.

6. Jot down one takeaway from the Lord God's encounter with Elijah. What do you find interesting, significant, or beneficial?

EMOTIONAL REST

Recall the three lies that Pastor Mike identified that lead to frequent burnout:

- It has to be perfect.
- I have to make everyone happy.
- It's fine. I'm fine.

1. What is one action you will take personally to begin to address each lie?

   Lie #1:

EMOTIONAL BURNOUT, EMOTIONAL REST

Lie #2:

Lie #3:

2. Read each of the following ten verses. Imagine you are experiencing emotional burnout (or maybe you currently are). What comfort or assurance does each verse provide for you personally? Then pick one verse and commit it to memory.

   Exodus 33:14: The LORD replied, "My Presence will go with you, and I will give you rest."

   Psalm 23:4: Even though I walk through the darkest valley, I will fear no evil, for you are with me; your rod and your staff, they comfort me.

Psalm 27:13: I remain confident of this: I will see the goodness of the Lord in the land of the living.

Psalm 34:19: The righteous person may have many troubles, but the Lord delivers him from them all.

Psalm 73:26: My flesh and my heart may fail, but God is the strength of my heart and my portion forever.

Isaiah 40:29: He gives strength to the weary and increases the power of the weak.

EMOTIONAL BURNOUT, EMOTIONAL REST

Isaiah 40:31: But those who hope in the Lord will renew their strength. They will soar on wings like eagles; they will run and not grow weary, they will walk and not be faint.

Matthew 6:34: "Therefore do not worry about tomorrow, for tomorrow will worry about itself."

Matthew 11:28: "Come to me, all you who are weary and burdened, and I will give you rest."

2 Corinthians 12:9: "My grace is sufficient for you, for my power is made perfect in weakness." Therefore I will boast all the more gladly about my weaknesses, so that Christ's power may rest on me.

PRAYER

Dear God, thank you for speaking the truth to me. It's not easy. It's not always convenient or popular, but it is good for souls. Everyone is at such different places. Some need a kick in the pants from you, and some need an arm around the shoulder to slow them down. I pray more than anything that you would help me also remember that through Jesus, I have an identity that can't be shaken. My worth and value are not in how much I produce but instead in what I have been given free of charge at the cross of your Son. Help my greatest joy not to be in my income, home, looks, or accomplishments but instead in everything that Jesus accomplished through his life, death, and resurrection. All of this is free of charge, by grace, and through faith.

Heavenly Father, I can picture marriages that are restored and kids who aren't anxious because there are a million things on their schedules. I can picture people lingering over open Bibles with a cup of coffee, having time to actually pray and realizing how beautiful and glorious you are. God, such things are possible when we stop sprinting and instead run this race of faith that you've called us to. Help me to get there by your grace and with your help. I pray this in the beautiful name of Jesus. Amen.

CONCLUDING THOUGHTS

Dr. Bruce Becker

REST. It's a vital component of God's designed rhythm for you and me.

The Old Testament Israelites lived without a rhythm of work and rest when they were slaves in Egypt. They had no days off for physical rest. They had no designated day for worshiping the Lord God. And slavery took an emotional toll on them as well. For decades, they lived without that rhythm of physical, spiritual, and emotional rest.

With the Exodus, however, the Lord God restored that rhythm when he made his covenant with his Old Testament chosen people. With *Shabbat*, God's people had weekly and yearly reminders of God's intended rhythm for their lives.

When Jesus left heaven and came to this earth, he came to offer us a better rest, a permanent rest. **"Come to me, all you who are weary and burdened, and I will give you** rest. **Take my yoke upon you and learn from me, for I am gentle and humble in heart, and you will find rest for your souls. For my yoke is easy and my burden is light"** (Matthew 11:28-30). It is the gospel, the good news of what Jesus has done for us, that gives rest to our souls.

As a result, we New Testament Christians no longer are required to observe a Sinai Sabbath Day. We have Jesus as our rest. In fact, the apostle Paul, in his letter to the Christians living in Colossae, reminded God's New Testament people that the Old Testament Sabbath was only a shadow, a picture of the coming Messiah: **"Therefore do not let anyone judge you by what you eat or drink, or with regard to a religious festival, a New Moon celebration or a Sabbath day. These are a shadow of the things that were to come; the reality, however, is found in Christ"** (Colossians 2:16,17). The Old Testament *Shabbat* was a picture pointing to Jesus the Christ, who is our true rest.

The writer to the Hebrew Christians, who knew all about *Shabbat*, gives us a final encouragement: **"There remains, then, a Sabbath-rest for the people of God; for anyone who enters God's rest also rests from their works, just as God did from his. Let us, therefore, make every effort to enter that rest"** (Hebrews 4:9-11). We don't find true rest from what we do or what we accomplish.

We find it in Jesus.

ABOUT THE AUTHORS

Pastor Mike Novotny pours his Jesus-based joy into his ministry as a pastor at The CORE (Appleton, Wisconsin) and as the lead speaker for Time of Grace, a global media ministry that connects people to God through television, print, and digital resources. He is unafraid to bring grace and truth to the toughest topics of our time and has taken on those topics in many books, podcasts, and videos. Mike lives with his wife, Kim, and their two daughters, Brooklyn and Maya; runs long distances; and plays soccer with other middle-aged men whose best days are long behind them.

Dr. Bruce Becker currently serves as the executive vice president for Time of Grace. He is a respected and well-known author, podcaster, and public speaker. He has served as the lead pastor of two congregations; as a member of several boards; and on many commissions, committees, and task forces. In 2012 he completed his professional doctorate in leadership and ministry management. Bruce and his wife, Linda, live in Jackson, Wisconsin. Find Dr. Becker's podcast, *Bible Threads With Dr. Bruce Becker*, at timeofgrace.org, Apple Podcasts, Spotify, and many other podcasting platforms or by scanning this code:

OTHER BOOKS BY MIKE

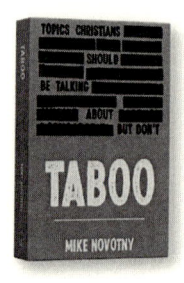

Taboo
Topics Christians Should Be Talking About but Don't

3 Words That Will Change Your Life
The Secret to Experiencing the Joy of God's Presence

When Life Hurts
How to See Through Suffering

You Know God Loves You, Right?

FIND THESE BOOKS AND MORE BY SCANNING THE CODE OR VISITING TIMEOFGRACE.STORE.

ABOUT TIME OF GRACE

Time of Grace is for people who are experiencing the highest of highs or have hit rock bottom or are anywhere in between. That's because through Time of Grace, you will be reminded that the One who can help you in your life, the God of forgiveness and grace and mercy, is not far away. He is right here with you. GOD is here! He will help you on your spiritual journey. Walk with us at timeofgrace.org.

TO DISCOVER MORE, PLEASE VISIT TIMEOFGRACE.ORG OR SCAN THIS CODE:

YOU CAN ALSO FIND OUT HOW TO WATCH *TIME OF GRACE* WITH PASTOR MIKE BY SCANNING THIS CODE:

HELP SHARE GOD'S MESSAGE OF GRACE

Every gift you give helps Time of Grace reach people around the world with the good news of Jesus. Your generosity and prayer support take the gospel of grace to others through our ministry outreach and help them experience a satisfied life as they see God all around them.

GIVE TODAY AT TIMEOFGRACE.ORG/GIVE,
BY CALLING 800.661.3311,
OR BY SCANNING THE CODE BELOW.

THANK YOU!